THE HELP MEET'S
Journey

Yearly companion
journal for

CREATED TO BE HIS HELP MEET

The Help Meet's Journey®
Copyright © 2007 by Michael and Debi Pearl
ISBN-13: 978-1-892112-87-3
ISBN-10: 1-892112-87-6
First printing: February 2007
Second printing: May 2007

Visit www.NoGreaterJoy.org for information on other products produced by No Greater Joy Ministries.

Requests for information should be addressed to:
No Greater Joy Ministries Inc. *1000 Pearl Road, Pleasantville, TN 37033 USA*

Cover photo by Erin Harrison
Cover design by Clint Cearley and Elizabeth Aprile
Model for cover photo, Shoshanna (Pearl) Easling, youngest of the Pearl children.
Interior layout by Lynne Hopwood

Printed in the United States of America

This is your Journey

Your stories, doodlings, studies, and pictures will become the camera of your soul recording a lasting memory of the miracle God is doing in you.

Don't be afraid. God is good. He is looking for someone to bless.

It is your turn.

Together we will look closely at what *God* has said to *women*.

For me and for hundreds of thousands of other women that moment of truth caused us to groan a sigh of surprise which, in the English language sounds like "WOW."

Then there comes the feeling of relief and a call from deep within, "Dear God help me."

This is the beginning of your journey.

*Spot for a photo of you
and your man*

This is us

Date

Begin your journey by listing the 10 most important things you would like to see change in your marriage.

_____

_____

_____

_____

_____

_____

_____

_____

For the man is not of the woman;

but the *woman of* the man.

Neither was the man created for the woman;

but the *woman for* the man.

I CORINTHIANS 11:8-9

 A WISE WOMAN DOESN'T TAKE ANYTHING FOR GRANTED. ❤

She is thankful to be loved and seeks to make herself more lovely.

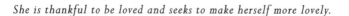

♥ TIME TO CONSIDER ♥

*God's perfect will for my life is that I be a help meet to
my husband. I do have a choice in how good my marriage will be.*

⟐ Make a new habit

Think of ways you can be a helper to your husband. Start today.

_____

_____

_____

_____

_____

✤ Getting Serious with God

Locate in Scripture (King James Bible) the following words or traits as they relate
to a woman of God. Write the verses here, and ask God to work each of these
attributes into your character.

   1. Virtue   *2. Graciousness*   *3. Wisdom*   *4. Prudence*   *5. Goodness*

_____

_____

_____

_____

_____

_____

_____

_____

_____

A Good Help Meet keeps her focus and passion to be of service first to her husband, second to her children and then to others. List new ways.

"Crown"

The word *crown* appears 62 times in the Bible. Look up the verses that contain the word *crown* and make a list of what crowns can be. For instance, grandchildren are crowns to the old man.

Proverbs 12:4 "A <u>virtuous woman is a crown</u> to her husband: but she that maketh ashamed is as rottenness in his bones."

How can you be a crown to your husband?

You will be doing a word study for some chapters. For those of you who have never done a word study, here is an example.

Definition of *Gladness*

Look up each verse where the word *gladness* appears in the Bible. From reading the context come up with an understanding of the definition of the word.

Gladness is defined in the Bible by its association with:

- Joy
- Shouting and singing
- Rejoicing and thanksgiving
- The voice of mirth and the voice of melody

Note that it is GOD that wants to HEAR gladness.

> Psalms 51:8 Make me to **hear** <u>joy and gladness</u>;

Note <u>who</u> should be glad and <u>what</u> a glad person does.

> Psalms 68:3 But let the *righteous* be glad; let them <u>rejoice</u> before God: yea, let them <u>exceedingly rejoice</u>.

> Isaiah 35:10 And the *ransomed of the LORD* shall return, and come to Zion with songs and everlasting <u>joy</u> upon their heads: they shall obtain <u>joy and gladness</u>, and <u>sorrow and sighing</u> shall flee away.

> Isaiah 51:11 Therefore the **redeemed of the LORD** shall return, and come with <u>singing</u> unto Zion; and everlasting <u>joy</u> shall be upon their head: they shall obtain <u>gladness and joy</u>; and <u>sorrow and mourning</u> shall flee away.

Note the consequences of the person who does not offer gladness to God.

> Deuteronomy 28:47-48 Because thou servedst not the LORD thy God with <u>joyfulness</u>, <u>and with gladness of heart</u>, for the abundance of all things; therefore shalt thou serve thine enemies which the **LORD shall send <u>against thee,</u>** in hunger, and in thirst, and in nakedness, and <u>in want of all things</u>: and he shall put a yoke of iron upon thy neck, until he have destroyed thee.

Secret Garden

Record your thoughts, feelings, hurts, joys and hopes.

Being his helper may be God's plan for improving his leadership 🖤

NOTES

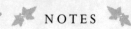

NOTES

A merry heart maketh a *cheerful countenance*:

but by sorrow of the heart

the spirit is broken.

PROVERBS 15:13

♥ THE JOY OF THE LORD IS MY STRENGTH ♥

❤ TIME TO CONSIDER ❤

God's perfect will is that I learn to be the best help meet *possible.*

🕊 Make a new habit

My husband is highly attracted to my smile. I want my husband to love me.
What can I do today that will make him smile?

_____

_____

_____

_____

🍃 Getting Serious with God

Write out the days of one week (Monday, Tuesday, Wednesday…). Make a daily
plan to practice joy and jot down any blessings that came from your joyful attitude.
Note the expressions on the faces of people you meet throughout the week. If you
could put words to their expressions, what would they be? If you get tempted to
be in a bad mood this week, stop, look in the mirror and think about what your
expression is saying to those around you. Play a game with your children one of
these days. Ask them to pretend to be "the mommy" when she is happy, then when
she is grumpy, or while doing chores have everyone first pretend to be grumpy
and move slowly around the house, then pretend to be happy and joyful. Make up a
new "happy" song to sing while you are working.

_____

_____

_____

_____

_____

_____

10   *God wants me to have a glow that will refresh my husband* ❤

"Joy"

Refer back to page 6 on how to do a word study. Look up each time the word *joy* is recorded in the Scripture. Organize verses into groups. What do you see that God is teaching us about joy?

A merry heart maketh a cheerful countenance ❤

Secret Garden

How did joy *change your family life this week? Where did you stumble?*
Purpose before God to deal daily with the "poor me" attitudes
quickly before they ruin the day.

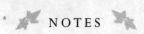

NOTES

NOTES

In every thing give thanks:
for this is the *will of God*
in Christ Jesus concerning you.

I THESSALONIANS 5:18

❤️ A WISE WOMAN SETS A JOYFUL MOOD IN HER HOME. ❤️

*Through laughter, music, and happy times, she creates a positive attitude
in her children. She knows that a light-hearted home
relieves her husband of stress.*

♥ TIME TO CONSIDER ♥

*God's perfect will for my life is that I be a help meet to
my husband. I do have a choice in how good my marriage will be.*

☆ Make a new habit

Go over the questions in the "Time to Consider" portion of the book. Holding
a grievance against your husband in your heart is an enemy of a thankful heart.
Throughout this week, purpose to challenge yourself with question #7- *Am I
willing to lay down my grievance toward my husband for the hope of a heavenly marriage?*
Record your victories.

Look for the daily miracles ♥

Getting Serious with God

Keep an old Bible in the bathroom and read some Philippians each trip. Look up Deuteronomy 28:47-48. Have you ever wondered why life seems hard on you? Why you are not blessed? God promises both blessings and cursings. What can you change in your life that might bring blessing?

I Peter 3:1-6

To whom is this passage addressed?

What is the first admonition? To be in...

To whom are you directed to be in subjection?

If you obey what reward might you have?

What actions of yours will God use to win your husband? By the ...

Does this include lost husbands?

What kind of countenance does God use?

What is the evidence of that countenance?

What woman in Scripture should we study to learn how to be a good help meet?

Ask God to take your irritations ♥

Secret Garden

What has God taught you concerning joy and thanksgiving?

Ask God for true love in your heart for others

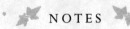

NOTES

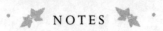

NOTES

CHAPTER 4 .... THANKSGIVING PRODUCES JOY ♥

MEMORY VERSE

*A*nd let them sacrifice the sacrifices of *thanksgiving*, and declare his works with *rejoicing*.

PSALM 107:22

LIVE WITH THANKSGIVING, FORGIVENESS, AND JOY,

and enjoy all your moments as if they were your last.

25

❤ TIME TO CONSIDER ❤

Traits of a good help meet: she is joyful, she makes love fun,
she is thankful and content.

Make a new habit

Think of ways to be a playmate to your husband.

Getting Serious with God

<u>Make a list</u> of ways that you can start showing thankfulness. Be creative in how you remind yourself and live out this list. (One hint: brainstorm practical ideas by yourself or with your children, write them out on slips of paper, put them in a box and each lunchtime, pull one out and practice).

"Jezebel"

Read I Kings 16 and II Kings 9. There are two women in Scripture that are there for our example. Sarah is the example of how to become a righteous wife and Jezebel is the example of how to not act. Look up and read the story of Jezebel. As you read, consider her different actions or reactions, then turn to the last reference of Jezebel-type ladies found in Revelation 2:20 and learn more of what not to be.

List some phrases that relate what Jezebel did or said that reveals her character and gives us clues in how not to act.

For example, I Kings 21:25, Jezebel stirred up Ahab.

Secret Garden

Having fun with your husband requires you to be able to laugh at yourself and be free to enjoy life's funny moments. Purpose before God to be light-hearted.

God's love and forgiveness can reach down and make you whole

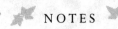

NOTES

Trust in the LORD, and do good;
so shalt thou dwell in the land, and verily
thou shalt be fed.

Delight thyself in the LORD;
and he shall give thee the desires of thine heart.

Commit thy way unto the LORD;
trust also in Him; and He shall bring it to pass.
And He shall bring forth thy righteousness
as the light, and thy judgment as the noonday.

Rest in the LORD, and wait patiently
for him: fret not thyself because of him who
prospereth in his way, because of the man who
bringeth forth wicked devices to pass.

Cease from anger, and forsake wrath:

Fret not thyself in any wise to do evil.

PSALM 37:3-8

♥ DO YOU HAVE ENOUGH FEAR OF GOD ♥
to not question His Word?

Today, you have <u>two choices</u> open to you. You can excuse yourself from responsibility by mentally assigning various excuses to your situation, or you can choose to believe God and become a 100% help meet regardless of anything that would stand in your way. Which will it be?

Write the answers to these questions from chapter 5.

1. What is the key to understanding our roles as wives?

2. Where are peace and joy found?

3. If your husband does not love you, does that negate your responsibility or prevent you from fulfilling your role?

4. What is the gift that God gives that will help you in your pursuit of becoming a help meet?

5. List three words that are part of the blueprint for help meets.

6. What can you do that will cause you to know God more and cause you to care about the things he cares about?

7. Are you committed to a heavenly marriage?

You serve Christ by serving your husband ♥

Getting Serious with God

To commit your way unto the Lord is to say, "Not my will, but thine, be done."
Read Psalm 37:3-8. Identify the positive action verbs (do this) and the negative
action verbs (don't do that) in these verses.

Ephesians 5:22-24

To whom is this passage addressed?

To whom are you to submit? Your pastor or your OWN husband? OWN seems like a redundant word, yet in like passages it is always included.

The word FOR tells you why you are to submit. What is the reason given?

What is the example given of why you are to submit to your OWN husband?

The word *therefore* signals that he is now coming to the conclusion of the matter. Write the conclusion in your own words.

Wisdom is not earned; it is a gift ♥

Secret Garden

God's Word is a powerful weapon against worried, fretful, angry thoughts.
Record how God is changing you.

NOTES

NOTES

THE FEAR OF THE
LORD
is the beginning of
WISDOM

PROVERBS 9:10A

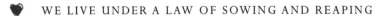

❤ WE LIVE UNDER A LAW OF SOWING AND REAPING ❤

that is as certain and unrelenting as disease and death.

♥ TIME TO CONSIDER ♥

Peace is a fruit of the Spirit. The fruit of the Spirit is not party to tension, stress, nervousness, uptightness, or bitterness.

Make a new habit

When you feel yourself beginning to have a critical spirit, stop, take a deep breath, silently ask for wisdom, then think of something that is on your thankful list. This is remolding a habit, and, in time, practice makes perfect. Record your results this week.

Getting Serious with God

Write out the definition for the word *odious*. Learn to hate the idea of ever being guilty of such a thing. Any time you are showing irritation and blame toward others, keep in mind that the earth is disquieted due to your being an odious, married woman.

True spirituality is obeying God's recorded Word

"Fear"

Look up the phrases "fear of God" and "fear of the Lord." How many times do they appear? What do you think God is trying to teach us? How differently would we react to our daily challenges if we truly feared God, if we feared his law of sowing and reaping?

Look up each verse and ask yourself how these verses can teach you to be a better help meet.

He that soweth iniquity reapeth vanity ♥

Secret Garden

Write out what God is doing in your heart through this study.

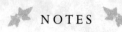

NOTES

*E*very *wise woman* buildeth her house: but the foolish plucketh it down with her hands.

PROVERBS 14:1

A WISE WOMAN IS ALWAYS LEARNING.

She is open to change. She is ready to hear. She pursues knowledge.

❤ TIME TO CONSIDER ❤

God had a plan for women from the beginning.
You are not an exception to his plan.

❦ Make a new habit

Think of the thing your husband does that irritates you the most. Now say to yourself, "I do not see the whole picture. I do not know what God is doing in my life or my husband's life. My critical attitude is a far graver sin than his bad habits. I am guilty of blaspheming the written Word of God when I do not love and obey my husband. Therefore, I am laying down my campaign against him concerning this issue. And, as far as I am concerned, it is God's business to direct my husband and convict him. I am trusting God." Record the results of this new habit here.

For as a man thinketh in his heart, so is he

Getting Serious with God

Go back through the previous story called *Alone*. Every time you read the word *"When"*, stop and ask yourself, *"When* my husband acts as her husband acted, do I react as she did?" Write your own new response to each *"When."* Ask God to give you the wisdom and courage to follow through on your new commitment. Write out your commitments here.

"Rejoice"

Rejoice is a beautiful word, full of hope, thanksgiving, contentment, and reward.

An antonym to *rejoice* is *regret*. *Regret* is one of the ugliest words in the human language. It is important to know that the word *regret* does not appear in the KJV Bible. God does not include it in his words to us. Regret offers no going back, no recovery, and no hope. It preys on the mind. It destroys our peace. It is continual shame. Many of us live in regret and it leaves us defeated, it steals our joy, and it causes us to lose our confidence that we are really forgiven. It is time we eliminate this word from our vocabulary and learn to rejoice in God's redemption for us.

The Bible is full of the word *rejoice*. Look up some of these verses and record when, why and how we are expected to rejoice. Let the Words of God come into your mind and soul. The Bible teaches us that the very Words of God are effectual, which means hearing and understanding the words will change how you feel and think.

"That the communication of thy faith may become effectual by the acknowledging of every good thing which is in you in Christ Jesus." Phm 1:6

As you read the verses containing the word *rejoice* God will be training you to rejoice! Use extra paper found at the back of the book if needed.

Secret Garden

What have you purposed to do with your 40,000 daily thoughts to be the help meet God intended you to be for your husband?

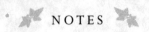

MEMORY VERSE

*B*e ye transformed by the *renewing* of your mind. ROMANS 12:1

♥ A WISE WOMAN LEARNS TO ADAPT TO HER HUSBAND ♥

♥ TIME TO CONSIDER ♥

Wisdom is knowing what you "bought" when you married that man, and learning to adapt to him as he is, not as you want him to be.

Who is *your* man?

Make a list of your husband's traits—things that indicate which of the three types he most expresses. It may be a combination, with one more dominant. Now, begin a list of things you can do that will set him free to be the man God made him to be.

Let your husband be the man God made him to be ♥

I Timothy 2:9-15

The Birth Promise

To whom is the passage addressed?

What is the first admonition concerning?

What is the description both in clothes and in attitude of how not to bring attention to our bodies?

If your profession is military, you wear a uniform. If your profession is of a woman who fears God then you are to dress accordingly. God calls dressing properly--

What does the Scripture indicate would include **good works?**
(Do a simple word study.)

Verses 11, 12, 13 and 14 address a woman's **silence**, **subjection** and **the reason why God demands** women concur with this rule.

Verses 11 & 12 God gives 5 ways women should act. He repeats and restates as if to make the point stick. List those 5 things.

Verses 13 & 14 God says why this rule is so important. Restate in your own words.

The first part of verse 15 God gives us the promise. He starts the promise with a heavy first word, *"Notwithstanding."* I looked up every time *notwithstanding* appears and wherever it appears I could have used the phrase, "I'm here to tell you something you can count on." Restate God's promise in your own words.

The second part of verse 15 God uses the big word *if*. God's promise is conditional. God sums up his discussion concerning his requirements (verses 9-15) to receive the promise with a short, concise conclusion. Remember he is addressing women. "They" is a pronoun referring back to women. Restate his conclusion in your own words.

The man you are married to is the right man 💙

Secret Garden

*What changes do you need to make in your thoughts and attitudes to be
a tailor-made help meet to your husband?*

NOTES

NOTES

MEMORY VERSE

nd the **LORD GOD** said,
It is not good that the man should
be alone; I will make him an
help meet for him.

GENESIS 2:18

FROM THE BEGINNING GOD MEANT FOR US TO BE

a comfort, a blessing, a reward, a friend, an encouragement,
and a right-hand woman.

God made us women to be help meets, and it is in our physical nature to be so.
It is our spiritual calling and God's perfect will for us.

Make a new habit

Is it God's will for your husband to adapt to you, or is it God's will for you
to adapt to him? What habits in your life <u>should you change</u> to adapt to your
husband's needs? Record your results this week. Sleep? Eating? Sports?

The way you think determines how you will feel ❤

The word *wisdom* appears 223 times in God's Word. As you look up and read each time the word *wisdom* appears, God will do a work in you and give you wisdom as you seek it. The Bible teaches that the sister of *wisdom* is God's commandments, and the kinswoman to *wisdom* is understanding (Prov. 7:4). Add to your diary your favorite *wisdom* verses. Establish one time each day that you will be reminded to ask God for wisdom. For instance, I have resolved for myself that when I stop at a red light, I will remember to pray for my husband. At every meal, we pray for both safety and *wisdom* for ourselves and our children. Write down a certain hour or occasion that will remind you to silently ask God for *wisdom* for yourself and for your husband.

Share your husband's dreams

Secret Garden

Life is full of choices. How you respond to the simple things
of life often decides your fate.
How has this chapter changed your fate?

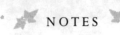

NOTES

NOTES

NOTES

Let this mind be in you, which was also in Christ Jesus.

PHILIPPIANS 2:5

She does not see herself as "God's gift to men;" therefore, she is joyful and content in her present circumstances.

You are what you think, and God tells you how to think: Think the truth.

Wisdom Test

1. Do you have enough fear of God to not question his Word?

2. Do you sometimes feel God is punishing you by telling you to obey your husband?

3. Would you give God excuses like, "My husband is mean," or, "I am a strong personality, and he is weak"?

4. How would you respond if God gave you directions on how to talk, when not to talk, or how to dress and even wear your hair?

5. Are you comfortable with dismissing the Bible's role for women by saying we live in a different culture?

6. When God says to reverence (meaning, stand in awe of) your husband, do you think that is demanding too much?

7. Will you say, "If God says it, or even suggests it, then that is what I will do"?

Getting Serious with God

Now that you have thought more about your role as a help meet, it is time to go back and add to the list of things you could be doing that will free your husband to be the man God created him to be.

Romans 12:1

To whom is the passage addressed?

List the 3 ways God tells us to present our bodies.

What would you change in your life that has conformed to the world?

The renewing of your mind was discussed in chapter 7. Remember reading *Stinking Thinking* on page 73? Have your 40,000 daily thoughts become those of rejoicing and praise?

Write some of the bad habits God has addressed in your life and given you victory over.

If someone came to you and said they really wanted to know God's will in their lives, from what you have just studied could you tell them what God's will in their life is?

Write your answer to them.

Remember the red suitcase ♥

Secret Garden

If you can say, "Not my will but thine, be done," then you can know that your prayer is based on the fear of God. It is the beginning of wisdom. Ask God to give you the beginning of wisdom by asking him to teach you to fear him.

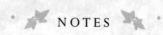

For Adam was first formed, then Eve.

And Adam was not deceived, but the

woman being deceived was in the transgression.

I TIMOTHY 2:13, 14

For a man indeed ought not

to cover his head, forasmuch

as he is the image and glory of God:

but the woman is the glory of the man.

1 CORINTHIANS 11:7

MAN WAS CREATED TO SUBDUE

Woman was created to assist

God placed man in the position of HEAD of the family, not because he is wiser or more capable, but because it is part of God's eternal design.

Make a new habit

When people think of your family, do they see your husband as the principal player, or do they think of you as the main character? Would they refer to your family as "Cathy's family" or as "John's family"? Have you usurped the position of headship? What can <u>you</u> do to reinforce the idea that your husband is the leader?

_____

_____

_____

_____

_____

_____

_____

_____

_____

_____

Getting Serious with God

The very first command God ever gave to a woman was, "Thy desire shall be to thy husband and he shall rule over thee" (Gen. 3:16). Is your desire toward your husband? Do you live to please him? Or, do you expect him to live up to your convictions and whims? Do you spend your days in angry frustration over his unwillingness to change to your specifications? If so, you have become a Jezebel. Write a letter to God asking Him for the strength and wisdom to have your desire be to your husband.

Profile Contrast

Look up these verses and restate them in your words.

Jezebel	Virtuous Woman
1. Prophetess - Rev. 2:20	1. Help Meet - Genesis 2:8
2. Teacher - I Timothy 2:9-15	2. Silent - I Corinthians 14:34
3. One who pities - I Kings 21:4-7	3. Encourager - I Peter 3:1-6
4. Religious - I Kings 16:31	4. Prudent Worker - Proverbs 31:10-31
5. Controller - I Timothy 2:6	5. Submissive - Colossians 3:18

A virtuous woman is hardworking ❤

Secret Garden

Compare the five qualities of the Jezebel Profile with the Virtuous Woman profile at the end of chapter 11. Where do you fit in? Ask God to make you into the Virtuous Woman you were meant to be.

NOTES

NOTES

For the husband is the head of the wife, even as Christ is the head of the church:

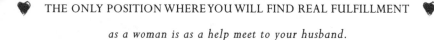

and he is the savior of the body. EPHESIANS 5:23

THE ONLY POSITION WHERE YOU WILL FIND REAL FULFILLMENT

as a woman is as a help meet to your husband.

♥ TIME TO CONSIDER ♥

God set up a chain of command, first in Heaven, and then again here
on earth. When you do not honor that command, you dishonor God, and apart
from repentance, you can expect to reap the sure consequences.

Make a new habit

Start thinking and acting as though your husband is the head of the company and
you are his secretary. What are some ways to help him in his managerial position?

_____

_____

_____

Getting Serious with God

Monday: Write three new things that you will add to your life that will cause you
to become more precious to your husband.

_____

_____

_____

Tuesday: List three things that you can do that will be a help to him.

_____

_____

_____

Wednesday: Write down three things you can do that will be an
encouragement to him.

_____

_____

The woman is the glory of the man ♥

Thursday: Jot down three ways you can change your appearance that he is sure to like.

_____

_____

_____

Friday: List three things you can do to your house that will please him.

_____

_____

_____

Saturday: Write three things you can do (for example, intimate time together) that will make him feel like he is THE MAN.

_____

_____

_____

Sunday: Plan three ways you can respond to him in front of others that will show a heart of respect and honor toward him.

_____

_____

_____

_____

_____

"Submit"

Find the definition of *submit*. Pick out 3 verses which deal with a woman submitting.

Secret Garden

Does your husband truly trust you? Are you truly precious to him?
Write a secret letter to him promising him a new woman.

What is more indecent than for a woman to quit her rank?

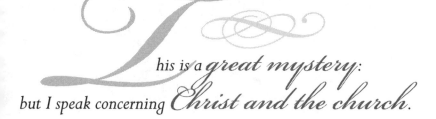

*his is a great mystery:
but I speak concerning Christ and the church.*

Nevertheless let every one of you in particular

so love his wife even as himself; and the

wife see that she reverence her husband.

EPHESIANS 5:32, 33

♥ A WISE WOMAN UNDERSTANDS THAT HER HUSBAND'S NEED ♥

*to be honored is not based on his performance, but on his nature and his
God-ordained position. She learns quickly to defer to his ideas or plans
with enthusiasm. She looks for ways to reverence him.
She knows this is God's will for her life.*

God admonishes us ladies to see that we reverence our man.

Make a new habit

Try to show your husband noticeable esteem at least three times a day. Plan small habits you can establish that will make it easier to remember to give him deference until it comes naturally. What will your plan be this week?

The word *REVERENCE* appears 13 times in God's Word. Eight occurrences have to do with reverencing men. Look up and consider each of these uses of the word *reverence*. As you read, you will understand from God's Word what God requires of you in reverencing your husband. Make a list of ways you have not shown reverence toward your husband, and then make a list of things you are going to start doing to correct them. Always keep in mind that, when you reverence your husband, you are reverencing God. *It is God's will for you to do this service to your husband.*

"Juana is a genuinely good woman. I honestly believe that she'd kill herself before she'd betray her husband. She's everything to him. She bears with him, humors him, mothers him-smiles through his tempers, his blackest moods. In fact, she's one of the rarest things on this earth—a wife."

"Rare?" Bruce said.

"Yes, rare. Because it's the hardest job in the world... Life asks a mighty heap of a woman..."

Bruce waited.

"Bring forth children in pain and sorrow. Remain mated to a creature who, in his essence, is half devil, and half child. Hold her tongue, because, tied up in a man, part, maybe, of the maleness of him, is a mule stubbornness that resents both advice and help. Settle down to dullness, when in her heart of hearts, every woman needs a little changefulness, excitement, glamour. Accept indifference and sometimes brutality instead of tenderness and romance. Even in the relationship which to a woman is a kind of glory, the expression of, and the culmination of love, she finds haste, the wolfish satisfaction of a mere physical appetite in her husband. God knows there must be times when a woman wonders if men really do have souls..."

From novel by Frank Yerby copyright 1955

Faith sees beyond the sinning husband to God who created us all

Secret Garden

Describe the change in your home, marriage and heart as you have committed to reverencing your husband.

MEMORY VERSE

or God hath not given us

the spirit of fear;

but of power, and of love,

II TIMOTHY 1:7 *and of a sound mind.*

A WISE WOMAN ALWAYS RECEIVES HER HUSBAND'S OVERTURES

with delight, no matter how clumsy he may be.

❤ Time to Consider ❤

The very heart of reverence is extreme appreciation and profound thankfulness that this man, just as he is, has chosen to love me, just as I am.

Make a new habit

Make a list of things you should do that will cause your husband to feel your honor, respect, and reverence. These might be simple things, like meeting him at the door when he comes home from work or reaching out to touch him in the car as you drive down the road. Practice what you have learned, and make a commitment to do these things, come sunshine or storm.

Deference to your man is the height of true femininity ❤

Getting Serious with God

It is time to make some written pledges to God about how you are going to stop reacting and start acting out being the help meet He meant for you to be. Don't record it until you have made up your mind it WILL be so.

"Mystery"

The word *mystery* appears 22 times in the Bible and only appears in the New Testament. Notice the different kinds of mysteries and what is the great mystery.

When you choose the right way, feelings will soon follow ♥

Here is where you stand alone with God letting Him know your prayers and inmost thoughts about what you have just studied in His Word.

It's all about Choices

*When God's choice (will) for your life becomes
your choice - things happen.*

The aged women likewise, that they
be in behaviour as becometh holiness,
not false accusers, not given to much wine,
teachers of good things; that they may teach
the young women to be

Sober,

to love their husbands, to love their children,
to be discreet, chaste, keepers at home, good,
obedient to their own husbands, that the word
of God be not blasphemed. TITUS 2:3-5

❤ A WISE WOMAN PATTERNS HER LIFE AFTER HER HUSBAND'S. ❤

His working, playing, eating, and sleeping habits become hers.

♥ Time to Consider ♥

A good help meet establishes a haven of rest. She will adjust to her husband's time schedule and eating habits. She will relax and enjoy her family, instead of worrying and fretting.

Make a new habit

Look up the words that God uses to describe a godless woman. Locate the verses in a concordance, and write them down. Ask God to cause you to HATE any sign of these things in your life. Believe and know that God <u>will</u> set you free.

- Foolish
- Clamorous
- Simple
- Knoweth nothing
- Like a swine (fat pig) with a gold nose-jewel
- Brawling
- Contentious
- Angry
- Odious
- Tattler
- Without discretion
- Wanders from house to house
- Stubborn
- Loud
- Busybodies

Getting Serious with God

Think of an occasion in the recent past when you became angry or were hurt because your husband responded in a way that you felt was wrong. Keep in mind that the other side of the coin of being angry is being hurt. It is one and the same coin, and it buys the same results: a bad marriage and a strained relationship. How different do you think the results might have been in your mind knowing that your job was to please that man? Write your own story. First, write the one that ended in a big fight, and next, write the story as it should have ended. Remember, he doesn't have to be right or kind for you to react in a godly way. This exercise will help you see the rationale for honoring your husband in a different light.

Simple planning can make all the difference 💜

Secret Garden

*Do you plan your daily life's happenings around what will please
and bless your man?*
*What can you implement in your daily life that will simplify
and improve your home?*

NOTES

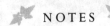

NOTES

MEMORY VERSE

The aged women likewise, that they be in behaviour as becometh holiness, not false accusers, not given to much wine, teachers of good things; that they may teach the young women to be sober, to *Love their husbands,* to love their children, to be discreet, chaste, keepers at home, good, obedient to their own husbands, that the word of God be not blasphemed. TITUS 2:3-5

A WISE WOMAN GAUGES HER HUSBAND'S NEEDS.

She seeks to fulfill his desires before even he is aware of them.
She never leaves him daydreaming outside the home.
She supplies his every desire.

The physical union between a man and a woman is so beautiful, so otherworldly that God uses sexual intercourse to illustrate our relationship with him (Ephesians 5:22-33).

Make a new habit

Make a list of personal plans of how you are going to love your husband. Be sure you come up with lots of bright ideas. I would suggest at least one special date a week. Plan on a different addition to your "birthday suit" each week such as: ribbons, bows, furs, jewelry, lace, jeans, scarves, feathers, ragged T-shirt, a chain of wild flowers, or whatever! Just use your imagination.

Getting Serious with God

The Song of Solomon is the 22nd book of the Bible. It is a love song/play that was written by Solomon about his wooing and wedding of a shepherd girl. All eight chapters tell the story (in graphic poetic detail) of longing for the lover, finding the lover, and what the lovers did when they were together. Most commentators find a need to turn the passage into a spiritual picture of Christ's love for the Church. I sincerely believe that old Solomon was thinking of the sexual expression of his love for her when he wrote it, and I think the same when I read it. What do you think? As you read God's novel about sex, ask yourself if you feel toward your husband the same hunger as the shepherd girl did for her lover. Make a written list of things you are going to do that will start a change in your actions. Your feelings will follow suit.

I Corinthians 7:3

Use a dictionary and record the definition of:

"render"

"due"

"benevolence"

Marriage means becoming one flesh ♥

Secret Garden

Good sex is now a holy obligation before God.
How is learning this going to change your actions?

NOTES

MEMORY VERSE

The aged women likewise, that they be in behaviour as becometh holiness, not false accusers, not given to much wine, teachers of good things; that they may teach the young women to be sober, to love their husbands, to *Love their children,* to be discreet, chaste, keepers at home, good, obedient to their own husbands, that the word of God be not blasphemed. TITUS 2:3-5

Your divine calling is to serve your family. True worship of God
is not dependent upon other people or special circumstances,
nor does it require a time of meditation.

Make a new habit

Look into your child's eyes and smile many times each day. Take a five-minute break every thirty minutes or so to just play with him or her. Never work alone; always have your "little buddy" helping you. Record a sweet story of how your child responded when you loved them with your smile.

Getting Serious with God

God directs us to train our children and, when necessary, to direct their path with correction. As women, we might feel we love our children too much to spank them. Our sentiment is silly and unloving. You cannot expect God's personal blessings on your life or on theirs unless you do it God's way. Study these verses and ask God to give you a heart of love and a backbone of courage to walk by his principles.

> **"He that spareth his rod hateth his son: but he that loveth him chasteneth him betimes"** (Proverbs 13:24).
>
> **"Foolishness is bound in the heart of a child; but the rod of correction shall drive it far from him"** (Proverbs 22:15).
>
> **"The rod and reproof give wisdom: but a child left to himself bringeth his mother to shame"** (Proverbs 29:15).

Record your weakest tendency concerning child training. Resolve it.

"Holy Children"

Many women reading Created to Be His Help Meet are in agony of spirit trying to decide whether to leave their husband or to stay with him, knowing that if they stay they are required by God to honor and obey him. Most of the women who have reached this point in their marriage have a valid reason for considering leaving. These few verses will help you find God's will concerning what you should do. Remember the last chapter where we studied how to know the will of God? Go back and reread what you learned in the study of Romans 12:1 & 2.

Rewrite each of the verses below. By rewriting each phrase in a verse, it seals it in your mind and you are much more likely to remember the context.

1 Corinthians 7:12

If any brother hath a wife that believeth not, and she be pleased to dwell with him, let him not put her away.

And the woman which hath an husband that believeth not, and if he be pleased to dwell with her, let her not leave him.

For the unbelieving husband is sanctified by the wife, and the unbelieving wife is sanctified by the husband: else were your children unclean; but now are they holy.

Secret Garden

How have you put your own "fun" before the good of your children?
Make some new commitments.

NOTES

NOTES

The aged women likewise, that they
be in behaviour as becometh holiness,
not false accusers, not given to much wine,
teachers of good things; that they may teach the
young women to be sober, to love their husbands,
to love their children, to be

Discreet,

chaste, keepers at home, good, obedient to
their own husbands, that the word of God
be not blasphemed. TITUS 2:3-5

♥ A WISE WOMAN DOESN'T ATTEMPT TO INSTRUCT HER HUSBAND ♥

*through feigned questions. Her questions will be sincere inquiries
concerning his will.*

♥ TIME TO CONSIDER ♥

A good help meet grows in grace and knowledge. She is gracious and honest. She is without guile toward her husband.

🕊 Locate in a concordance

Locate in a concordance every time the following words are used. Mark the words that describe you. Beside the words where you know you are lacking, put an X. Write out beside each word what you are going to start doing that will bring you closer to becoming what God desires.

- Chaste
- Sober
- Modest
- Shamefacedness
- Meek
- Gentleness

- Quiet spirit
- In subjection
- Obedient
- Kind
- Virtuous

- Prudent
- Good
- Discreet
- Keeper at home
- Gracious

136

Getting Serious with God

Do not be deceived. If you regularly use people as baby-sitters, visit around too often, ask for rides here and there, or frequently borrow other people's things, they might tolerate your selfishness, but they will never really like you. You will be secretly spoken of as a nuisance instead of a friend. Ask yourself what your family and friends would say about you in this area. Write your answer here.

A gracious woman retaineth honour

Secret Garden

What has God taught you this week? Tell Him.

A good help meet is without guile toward her husband

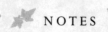

The aged women likewise, that they be in behaviour as becometh holiness, not false accusers, not given to much wine, teachers of good things; that they may teach the young women to be sober, to love their husbands, to love their children, to be discreet,

Chaste,

keepers at home, good, obedient to their own husbands, that the word of God be not blasphemed. TITUS 2:3-5

♥ A CHASTE WOMAN IS A MODEST WOMAN. ♥

God speaks of a woman maintaining her chastity and purity by the clothes she wears.

❤ TIME TO CONSIDER ❤

She who has ears...LET her hear!

The appearance of a Good Help Meet

Think with me one moment about the last time you went to church. In your mind's eye, scan the room and reflect on how the women, including yourself, were dressed. Now read what God says and rewrite in your own words:

"In like manner also, that women adorn themselves in <u>modest apparel</u>, with <u>shamefacedness</u> and <u>sobriety</u>; <u>not with broided hair, or gold, or pearls, or costly array</u>; But (which becometh women professing godliness) with good works. Let the woman learn in silence with all subjection. But I suffer not a woman to teach, nor to usurp authority over the man, but to be in silence. For Adam was first formed, then Eve. And Adam was not deceived, but the woman being deceived was in the transgression. {A Promise} *Notwithstanding she shall be <u>saved in childbearing</u>, if they continue in faith and charity and holiness with sobriety*" (I Tim 2:9-15).

144

Clothes speak to all who see us

Getting Serious with God

II Samuel 11 tells the story of how David sinned with Bathsheba. The last verse of that chapter reads, "But the thing that David had done displeased the Lord." Read the story found in II Samuel 11 & 12 and David's cry of repentance found in Psalm 51. Let the story of the misery of sin instruct you, change you, and cause you to desire to dress in a way that would never cause a brother in the Lord to lust. Make a list of clothes you are going to "throw out" for God's glory.

"Chaste"

God takes lusting very seriously. Women do not have the same struggle men have. A woman's sexual response kicks in in an aggressive way only after some time of physical contact. Once a woman begins to respond she has to struggle to resist. A man can be busy working through his taxes with his mind totally consumed with the matters at hand when a young woman comes into the room plops down in a chair and crosses her long uncovered legs in front of him. His physical response is immediate. His body responds before his brain or spirit has had time to assess the problem. This little sweetie would be shocked if she had any idea Mr. Old Frog had any sexual response to her. She would laugh at his discomfort. Yet, someday she will stand in the judgment for this occasion. Mr. Old Frog may avert his eyes and ask God to help him. Even though his body responded, he was victorious in his turning away from sin. Miss Sweetie will not be so lucky. Rewrite each line in your own words and ask God to help you not be guilty of this grave sin.

Matthew 5:27-30

Ye have heard that it was said by them of old time, Thou shalt not commit adultery:

But I say unto you, That whosoever looketh on a woman to lust after her hath committed adultery with her already in his heart.

And if thy right eye offend thee, pluck it out, and cast it from thee: for it is profitable for thee that one of thy members should perish, and not that thy whole body should be cast into hell.

And if thy right hand offend thee, cut it off, and cast it from thee: for it is profitable for thee that one of thy members should perish, and not that thy whole body should be cast into hell.

Secret Garden

Someday we will all give an account on the things done in
(or worn on) the body. (2 Cor. 5:10)
Record here how God has changed your heart and attitude
about yourself. This will reflect on how you dress.

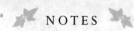

NOTES

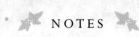

NOTES

The aged women likewise, that they
be in behaviour as becometh holiness,
not false accusers, not given to much wine,
teachers of good things; that they may teach the
young women to be sober, to love their husbands,
to love their children, to be discreet, chaste,

Keepers at home,

good, obedient to their own husbands,
that the word of God be not blasphemed.

TITUS 2:3-5

🖤 A HOME IS NOT A HOME UNLESS THE LADY IS THERE 🖤

♥ TIME TO CONSIDER ♥

A young mother's place is in the home, keeping it, guarding it, watching over those entrusted to her.

Make a new habit

Make your own list of traits of a good help meet.

Getting Serious with God

List things you can do that will make you more of a "keeper" of your home.

"Hospitality"

Hospitality is one way that a keeper at home can minister to others. Four times in his Word, God admonishes us to use hospitality in service to others. Look up those four verses, and seek ways to show hospitality to others.

"Use hospitality one to another without grudging" (I Peter 4:9).

Be frugal in all your endeavors ♥

Secret Garden

Your heart's prayer.

The aged women likewise, that they
be in behaviour as becometh holiness,
not false accusers, not given to much wine,
teachers of good things; that they may teach the
young women to be sober, to love their husbands,
to love their children, to be discreet, chaste,
keepers at home, *Good,*
obedient to their own husbands,
that the word of God be not blasphemed.

TITUS 2:3-5

♥ A GOOD WOMAN IS GENUINE, JOYFUL, VIRTUOUS, VALUABLE, ♥

competent, ready, kind, benevolent, merciful, hardworking, agreeable,
pleasant, congenial, honorable, faithful, gracious, and wise.

He was not created to be your servant.
You were created to be his helper, so get to it.

♥ Make a new habit

List the things that need fixing or completing around your home. What is one project that you and the children can learn to do together? Make a plan here and record your results.

Getting Serious with God

An excellent help meet's traits are listed in Proverbs 31. Go verse by verse and list your qualifications in reference to the Proverbs lady's.

"Gracious"

The word *gracious* appears 33 times in the Bible. Look up the words that appear in conjunction with gracious. Then look up the definition of *gracious* in a dictionary.

Secret Garden

What has God done to make you into a Proverbs 31 lady?

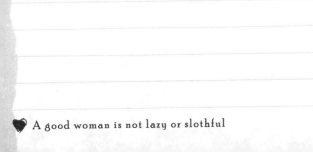

A good woman is not lazy or slothful

NOTES

The aged women likewise, that they
be in behaviour as becometh holiness,
not false accusers, not given to much wine,
teachers of good things; that they may teach the
young women to be sober, to love their husbands,
to love their children, to be discreet,
chaste, keepers at home, good,
Obedient to their own husbands,
that the word of God be not blasphemed.

TITUS 2:3-5

A WISE WOMAN HONORS GOD BY SUBMITTING TO HER HUSBAND.

*It is her God-appointed office that renders her second
in command in the family.*

❤ TIME TO CONSIDER ❤

The Scripture clearly teaches that a woman is to obey her own husband.

❧ Make a new habit

Emphatic Statements from God concerning Women

Look up the verses that contain the statements below, and mark them in your Bible. Will you obey God? Mark the emphatic statements that indicate you have been dishonoring to God, and ask God to help you as you start your path to obedience. Rewrite each phrase.

• Younger women, bear children.

• Younger women, guide the house.

• Wives, give none occasion to the adversary to speak reproachfully.

• Wives, submit to your own husbands.

• Wives, love your own husbands.

• Wives, love your children.

• Women, be discreet.

• Women, be chaste.

• Women, be keepers at home.

• Women, be sober.

God is a master at making heavenly marriages ❤

- Women, be good.

- It is a shame for a woman to be shorn or shaven.

- Woman's long hair is her glory and her covering.

- Women praying uncovered are not comely.

- Let the woman learn in silence.

- I suffer not a woman to teach.

- Women, do not usurp authority over the man.

- Wives, reverence your own husbands.

- Wives, have chaste conversation.

- Women, adorn yourselves in modest apparel.

- Women, have shamefacedness and sobriety.

- Let your adorning be the hidden man of the heart.

- Wives, have a meek and quiet spirit.

- Wives, render due benevolence to your husband.

- Wives, care how you may please your husbands.

- Women, keep silence in the churches.

- Women are not permitted to speak in church.

- Wives, be not idle.

- Wives, do not wander about from house to house.

- Wives, do not be tattlers or busybodies.

No pastor or minister is higher than your husband

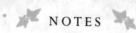

NOTES

MEMORY VERSE

*ikewise, ye wives, **be in subjection***
*to your **own husbands**;*

THAT, IF ANY OBEY NOT THE WORD,

*they also may **without the word** be won*

*by the **conversation** of the wives*

1 PETER 3:1

 ALL AUTHORITY IS DERIVED FROM GOD

*and must answer to him, but he has delegated some authority
to angels, some to government, some to the church,
some to husbands, and some to wives.*

♥ TIME TO CONSIDER ♥

A wife does not have to choose between God and her husband.
Render therefore unto your husband the things that are your husband's
and unto God the things that are God's.

Traits of a Good Help Meet

Go over this section at the end of chapter 23. Which trait do you need to work on?

_____

_____

_____

_____

_____

Getting Serious with God

Go through your Bible and find all the Scripture that we covered on the subject of <u>authority</u>. Ask God to give you a heart willing to cheerfully do his will, regardless of the immediate benefits.

_____

_____

_____

_____

_____

_____

_____

_____

_____

_____

God made the man the head of the woman ♥

You are not your husband's conscience 🖤

"Fruit of the Spirit"

Look up Galatians 5:22-23. Look up 2 verses for each of the fruits of the Spirit.

Secret Garden

Record your own story.

eirs together in the grace of life.

1 PETER 3:7c

A WISE WOMAN SEEKS TO BE PART OF HER HUSBAND'S LIFE.

His interests become her interests. She looks for ways to help him in all his endeavors. When he needs a helping hand, it is her hand that is there first.

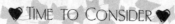

Who and what would my husband be if he had married another woman?
Have I made it possible for him to be a strong, confident,
aggressive man of God? Write your commitment.

NOTES

Be an encourager

177

"Heirs Together in the Grace of Life"

Look up 1 Peter 3:7 and Titus 3:7. Rewrite each phrase into your own words.

Believe God like Sarah ♥

Secret Garden

How has God changed you? Go back to the list you recorded at the beginning of this journey. Record the changes that have taken place in your spirit, your marriage and your home as a result of studying God's Word.

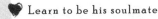

*Spot for a new photo of you
and your man*

This is a new photo of us

*Make this Journey again
this time next year...*

Be his friend 🖤

How has God changed you?

Go back to the list of ten things you recorded at the beginning of this book. Where you were once ignorant of God's plan, now you have the truth concerning your role as a help meet. Nothing will ever be the same. Fear God.

Plan for him

NOTES

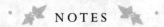

NOTES

NOTES